I0693600

Conduct Disorder:

Developmental, Physiological, Psychological, Sociological Factors and Treatment

Conduct Disorder

DSM-V

Conduct disorder (CD) behaviors are primarily present in children and adolescents. A recurring and persisting pattern of antisocial, hostile, or defiant conduct characterizes CD. The associated behaviors are not the social norm and infract developmentally appropriate societal expectations and rules (Mohan et al., 2023). CD is a disruptive behavior disorder.

CD diagnosis involves three criteria (A, B, and C). Criterion A defines CD as a repetitive and insistent pattern of conduct where the rights of others or developmentally appropriate societal norms or rules are violated and is shown by the existence of three (or more) criteria within 12 months, with a minimum of one criterion present within six months (American Psychiatric Association, 2022). Behavior patterns must be persistent.

Next, criterion B involves deficiency measures in social, educational, or work-related abilities. For individuals 18 years and older, a finding of CD can be concluded only if the criteria for antisocial personality disorder (ASPD) (criterion C) is not determined (American Psychiatric Association, 2022). CD can be comorbid.

Further, determinants for diagnosis include lack of remorse, lack of guilt, shallow effects, absence of prosocial emotions, and lack of effort to meet expectations (APA, 2022). CD diagnosis requires thorough evaluation and assessment. In summary, CD diagnosis is typically assigned to children and adolescents that have not reached aged 18. The individuals consistently and relentlessly disregard the rights of others and fail to conform their behavior to regulations or social norms appropriate for their age.

Signs/Symptoms

CD covers behaviors including troublemaking, such as disorderly, unruly, aggression, stealing, and lying. It also includes an opposition or lack of ability or failure to complete schoolwork, lack of positive relations or communications with adults, non-compliance with instructions, low self-esteem, poor social skills, no regard for standard rules, and emotional instability (Mohan et al., 2023). There are four broad categories of symptoms. The categories of symptoms are violence or aggression, destruction, deceit, and violation of rules. Consequently, the continuation of these behavior patterns into adulthood advances to ASPD (Mohan et al., 2023). Further, when signs and symptoms are present during development, it is necessary to differentiate between normal and pathological behavior.

Also, isolated dissocial behaviors or rule violations do not adequately support a CD diagnosis. There must be a distinguishing between delinquency and

CD (Mohan et al., 2023). An occasional rebellious act and a tendency to dispute and be disobedient are common behaviors experienced during development and may not be factors indicating CD (requires analysis of behavior patterns) (Mohan et al., 2023). Delinquency is not a disorder.

It is shown that assertive and defiant behaviors are essential to normalcy in children and ensure physical and social existence. Disruptive behaviors are seen to a certain extent in child and adolescent development (Gatti et al., 2019). Disruptive behaviors that develop into significant recurrent, callous, and relentless actions and that cause tribulation and disfunction are clinically significant (Mohan et al., 2023). Other signs and symptoms within the range of behaviors include misconduct and disobedience and behaviors such as yelling, tantrums, physical destructiveness and physical violence, bullying, and, more recently, cyberbullying.

Moreover, symptoms of CD are shown to chiefly evolve at an earlier age in boys than girls. For boys, the typical age CD symptoms present is about is between the ages of 10 and 12 and age 14-16 years for girls (Sagar et al., 2019). Further, CD (early on-set) is significantly associated with a substantial decline in educational accomplishment. By adolescence, individuals become at risk of socially isolating and developing an inclination towards drug use and abuse and criminal acts (Sagar et al., 2019). Adverse effects can continue into adulthood, resulting in poor outcomes.

Developmental Factors

Behavior patterns that encroach upon the rights of others and developmentally appropriate standards are characteristic of children and adolescents with CD. Subsequently, CD is also linked to adverse outcomes after reaching maturity, including substance abuse, lawbreaking, health problems, lower educational attainment, and patterns of unemployment (Tesli et al., 2024). CD diagnosis presents a three-fold increased probability of child mortality (Tesli et al., 2024). Individuals with early onset have lower IQ, inadequate verbal skills, and deficiency in executive functioning in contrast to children who develop CD at a later age. Attention deficits problems and problems with impulsivity are also more prevalent in children with early onset (Tesli et al., 2024). The CD presents a broad range of developmental challenges.

Additionally, problems with cooperating and sharing and the likelihood of having adversative living conditions is prevalent in children with CD. Their parents are likelier of having lower incomes than the median, more probable of having substance use disorders, have depressive disorders, and more probable of experiencing ASPD, which are all factors that can influence CD (Gatti et al., 2019). Further, developmental changes occur during the disorder. For example, as the child ages, instances of fighting may decrease, and instances of skipping school may increase.

Parents experiencing psychopathology, together with strict childrearing, is linked to CD. The manifestation of dissocial behavior in children is linked with parental support, parental sensitivity to the child, and punishment given during development (Özbay et al., 2024). Also, regular marital conflicts and violence between parents predict adolescent antisocial behavior. Further, problematic dispositions and behaviors that can contribute CD development (Özbay et al., 2024).

Influences and behaviors are observed characteristically

in early childhood.

Physiological Factors

Heredity, neuroanatomic factors, neurochemical factors, autonomic nervous system stimuli, prenatal and perinatal complications, and neurotoxins present as physiological factors associated with the causation of CD. Brain damage can influence normal function and present as a physiological factor associated with the causation of CD also (Sagar et al., 2019). Findings have shown distinct brain structure and behavior associated with CD.

Injury to the anterior division of each cerebral hemisphere (frontal lobe) has been connected to CD. The structure modulates cognition, emotions, and memory (Sagar et al., 2019). It also builds social relationships and personality (Sagar et al., 2019). The frontal lobe in CD may not function properly, causing, for example, a lack of empathy, acting without considering consequences, reduced executive function, and development of learned helplessness (negative stimuli and experiences are not causing change) (Sagar et al.,

2019). Frontal lobe impairment may be hereditary or due

to damage or injury. In addition, head injuries, even

minor, during developmental stages of childhood have

been linked to a high percentage of CD between ages 10

and 13 (Sagar et al., 2019). Further, personality traits

seen in CD are inheritable.

Brain imaging technique such as magnetic

resonance imaging (MRI) has been used to distinguish

structural brain variances between children with CD and

control groups. Researchers have found undersized brain

structures, reduced neural activity, reduced neural

response during moral processing and reduced cerebral

function in children with CD (Özbay et al., 2024).

Irregularities are mainly found in individuals with CD in

the right striatum, the insular lobe, the amygdalae, the

posterior-media aspect of the parietal lobule, and the left

medial-superior frontal gyrus (Özbay et al., 2024). These abnormalities are well documented.

Additionally, higher blood plasma serotonin levels influence antagonistic behavior in children. Capriciousness, aggression, and vehement conduct are linked to modulating action of specific brain regions. Structures associated with and influenced by high blood plasma levels are the amygdala, hippocampus, thalamus, hypothalamus, cingulate gyrus, basal ganglia, prefrontal cortex, and the orbitofrontal cortex (Sagar et al., 2019). Also note that serotonin was linked to aggression and impulsivity studies showed that serotonin deficiency is shown in individuals with impulse control and behavior disorders (Özbay et al., 2024). Serotonin transmits signals between nerve cells.

Moreover, unambiguous evidence has shown a link between the age of the mother at gestation and the probability of CD development in the offspring.

Research showed that pregnancy before age 18 is significantly linked to the extent of symptoms of CD in male children aged six through thirteen (Özbay et al., 2024). In addition, when the mother had a history of CD, there was a higher risk of adolescent or teenage pregnancy (Özbay et al., 2024). Further, the mother's lifestyle was also an influential factor.

Additionally, cerebral development in the fetus can be affected by substances. Specifically, psychotropic substance uses during certain stages of prenatal development can lead to lasting and sustained effects on the offspring's neuro-behavioral potential (Özbay et al., 2024). Also, in the same context, research has reliably evidenced that the children of mothers who consume nicotine during gestation are more probable of developing CD (Özbay et al., 2024). CD occurrence in children of mothers who smoked during pregnancy was more prevalent in boys.

Further, in the context of drinking during pregnancy, physical and neurological problems are prevalent. CD symptoms are severe when fetal alcohol syndrome is diagnosed (Özbay et al., 2024). In addition, studies have shown that moderate levels of alcohol exposure during pregnancy significantly increases the prevalence of CD (Özbay et al., 2024). Pregnancy is a critical time of development.

Psychological Factors

The causation and behavior problems associated with CD can be understood and addressed by various psychological theories. Deficits in reinforcement learning (RL) from discipline and less consistent reaction to reward has been associated with CD and other disorders (Elster et al., 2024). RL can help to understand deficits in decision making associated with CD.

Attachment theory suggests that interferences in or lack of parent-child bonding or attachment insecurity can lead to CD. Current research supports a relationship between insecure attachments and the psychopathology of CD (Sagar et al., 2019). Attachment mediates effective regulation. Deficits in emotional functioning are experienced with insecure attachment (risks for CD) (Sagar et al., 2019). Next, the coercive cycles theory posits how parents and caregivers can reinforce negative behaviors in children, creating a cycle of negativity (Gatti et al., 2019). Strict punishment during kindergarten through first and second grades predicted higher adolescent CD symptoms (Goulter et al., 2019). Moreover, children with a defiant temperament are punished harshly. Subsequently, the children are socialized to become aggressive, in which a bidirectional relationship is developed that supports additional adverse parent-child exchanges (Goulter et al., 2019). The coercive cycles are a vital mechanism underpinning aggressive behaviors.

CD has also been shown to be linked to deficit pathways in social information processing. Social cues may become misinterpreted, which can increase aggressive behaviors (Sagar et al., 2019). Research shown that disruptive behavior disorders and dysfunctional behaviors are linked to deficits in the ability to implement the sequential steps involved in social information processing (Martel, 2019). Studies examining the number of cues encoded about routine social problems have shown that violent children (school aged and adolescent) encode less cues in contrast to children with intermediate aggression or non-aggressive children and that children with identified disruptive behavior problems encode less cues than normal children (Martel, 2019). Research examining how children construe the cues in social situations showed that violent children were more prone to impute antagonistic intent when interpreting social situations in contrast to children who are aggressive or children who are non-aggressive (Martel, 2019). Also, studies shown that aggressive children contrast in their construction of alternative resolutions to problems that affect society and may make decisions that will further their aggressive behaviors (Martel, 2019). These theories collectively provide insights into the underlying mechanisms contributing to

the behavioral challenges observed in children with CD.

Sociological Factors

Sociological influences exist that may lead to CD development. These factors include under-resourced, poverty, disorganized neighborhoods, poor schools, and peer rejection (Özbay et al., 2024). Also, factors interrelated to family and social dynamics are linked to CD in young adulthood. Too, negative environmental effects are significantly influential because they are often systematized, extensive, and linked to additional determinant conditions. Extreme impoverishment is associated with multiple predisposing factors (Özbay et al., 2024). For example, extreme parenting practices in disadvantaged households can shape child behavior outcomes because of multiple risk factors.

Antisocial children disproportionally come from low socioeconomic status families. Low socioeconomic status, low family income, and low parental education predicted children with CD. In another study, low socioeconomic status predicted the onset of CD (Özbay et al., 2024). Also, family dependency on welfare benefits was distinctive in boys with CD (Özbay et al., 2024). Children and adolescents must develop self-regulation and coping mechanisms to help circumvent influences.

Communities have indirect effects on antisocial behavior through individuals and families. In a study, the relationship between community structure characteristics (concentrated poverty, racial divergency, economic sources, and violent crime percentage) and violence was mediated by parenting methods, gang participation, and peer violence (Özbay et al., 2024). Additionally, exposure to substance use and the prevalence of substance use in the community have also been shown to be significantly associated with the development of CD (Özbay et al., 2024). Obtainability of drugs and increased criminality in the community increases the risk of children developing CD (Özbay et al., 2024).

Accordingly, other sociological influences encompass nurture, child neglect, stressors, and coping mechanisms.

Research data suggests that schooling experiences need to be considered when evaluating risk factors for CD. Factors such as truancy, rudeness at school, and academic failure have all been associated with CD (Özbay et al., 2024). After children show signs and symptoms of both ADHD and early-onset CD, they are incredibly likely to fail at school (Özbay et al., 2024). The child's logic and rationality become impacted.

Moreover, in summary, the possibility of CD is greater in situations whenever the child is neglected, abused sexually or physically, and where there is use or dependence on drugs. Also, studies have shown that relationships with defiant peers predict CD, and the occurrence of CD is greater in communities increased occurrences of violence (Özbay et al., 2024).

Sociological factors are essential for improving
outcomes.

Treatment

The outlook of CD can differ. CD may resolve with maturity; however, with certain individuals, CD may endure, and these individuals may progress into ASPD and subsequently drug abuse (Özbay et al., 2024). Also, when CD is comorbid with ADHD, dissocial and violent behaviors are utmost prevalent (Özbay et al., 2024). Efficacious treatment outcomes can be accomplished using multidimensional approaches that target the school, household, and community where challenging behaviors ensue. Further, the multidimensional approaches include social skills training, cognitive behavioral therapy (CBT), evidence-based psychosocial treatments, parent management training (PMT), and pharmacological approaches (Mohamed et al., 2022). Medications used for CD are antipsychotic drugs, antidepressant drugs, central nervous system stimulants, and benzodiazepines (Özbay et al., 2024). No medications are formally approved for CD treatment. Medications are prescribed for symptoms.

The significance of treating CD is highlighted in the research. Intervention approaches must be implemented with respect to the age groups of children and adolescents (Sagar et al., 2019). Interventions are more effectual when beginning at age six and continuing until about eleven years of age. These approaches are suggested to be CBT approaches (Sagar et al., 2019). For adolescence-onset conduct disorder, treatment approaches may involve partial hospitalization programs and community-based methods (Sagar et al., 2019). Age-appropriate treatment and interventions are required for essential outcomes.

Moreover, research has shown that children in middle teenage years and older may not progress amply through typical treatment approaches. Consequently, increasing the ability to mentalize with mentalization-based treatment (MBT) was developed for adolescents that may not benefit from typical treatment programs (Hauschild et al., 2022). According to the MBT framework, deficits in the ability to mentalize are causal factors of aggressive demeanors behaviors (Hauschild et al., 2022). CD is a disorder that is problematic and adversely impacts children, families, and societies, and a multidimensional approach is posited for treatment.

Further, treatment outcomes are critical. Deficits in cognitive abilities and history of a dysfunctional family that may include ongoing parental criminal behavior can be indicators of a negative outcome (Mohan et al., 2023). Additionally managing nonadherence children can be challenging. Treatment approaches can be developed tailored based on age and comorbidities; however, research has shown that maintaining compliance remains difficult with children experiencing CD (Mohan et al., 2023). Subsequently, a significant number of individuals with CD remain non-compliant to treatment protocols (Mohan et al., 2023). Overtime, circumstances such as confinement can lead individuals to required or imposed treatment.

In conclusion, CD is linked to specific brain regions that facilitate the regulation of behavior, impulse control, and emotions. The specific cause of CD remains however, it has been evidence to result from a combination of biological, hereditary, environmental, psychological, and sociological influences. Psychopharmacology treatments may sometimes be recommended for severe CD, but not frequently. In detrimental situations when medication is prescribed for CD, it is for treating symptoms.

References

American Psychiatric Association. (2022). *Diagnostic and statistical manual of mental disorders* (5th ed., text rev.). https://doi.org/10.1176/appi.books.978089 0425787

Elster, E. M., Pauli, R., Baumann, S., De Brito, S. A., Fairchild, G., Freitag, C. M., & Kohls, G. (2024). Impaired punishment learning in conduct disorder. *Journal of the American Academy of Child & Adolescent Psychiatry*, *63*(4), 454-463. https://doi.org/10.1016/j.jaac.2023.05.032

Gatti, U., Grattagliano, I., & Rocca, G. (2019). Evidence-based psychosocial treatments of conduct problems in children and adolescents: An overview. *Psychiatry, Psychology and Law*, *26*(2), 171-193. https://doi.org/10.1080/13218719.2018.1485523

GBD 2019 Mental Disorders Collaborators. (2022).

Global, regional, and national burden of 12

mental disorders in 204 countries and territories,

1990–2019: A systematic analysis for the Global

Burden of Disease Study 2019. *The Lancet

Psychiatry, 9*(2), 137-150.

https://doi.org/10.1016/s2215-0366(21)00395-3

Goulter, N., McMahon, R. J., Pasalich, D. S., & Dodge,

K. A. (2019). Indirect effects of early parenting

on adult antisocial outcomes via adolescent

conduct disorder symptoms and callous-

unemotional traits. *Journal of Clinical Child &

Adolescent Psychology, 49*(6), 930–942.

https://doi.org/10.1080/15374416.2019.1613999

Hauschild, S., Kasper, L., Volkert, J., Sobanski, E., &

Taubner, S. (2022). Mentalization-based

treatment for adolescents with conduct disorder

(MBT-CD): A feasibility study. *European Child*

& *Adolescent Psychiatry, 32*(12), 2611–2622.

https://doi.org/10.1007/s00787-022-02113-4

Lahousen, T., Unterrainer, H. F., & Kapfhammer, H. P.

(2019). Psychobiology of attachment and

trauma: Some general remarks from a clinical

perspective. *Frontiers in Psychiatry, 10.*

https://doi.org/10.3389/fpsyt.2019.00914

Martel, M. M. (2019). Theories of oppositional defiant

disorder. *The Clinician's Guide to Oppositional

Defiant Disorder*, 31–42.

https://doi.org/10.1016/b978-0-12-815682-

7.00003-3

Mohamed, S. M., Marzouk, S. A., Ahmed, F. A.,

Nashaat, N. A. M., & Omar, R. A. E. A. T.

(2022). Cognitive behavioral program on

aggression and self-concept among

institutionalized children with conduct disorder.

Archives of Psychiatric Nursing, 39, 84–90.

https://doi.org/10.1016/j.apnu.2022.03.012

Mohan, L., Yilanli, M., & Ray, S. (2023). *Conduct disorder*. StatPearls.

Özbay, A., Özçelik, O., & Kahraman, S. (2024). Conduct disorder: An update. *Psikiyatride Güncel Yaklaşımlar, 16*(1), 72-87. https://doi.org/10.18863/pgy.1331287

Sagar, R., Patra, B., & Patil, V. (2019). Clinical practice guidelines for the management of conduct disorder. *Indian Journal of Psychiatry, 61*(8), 270. https://doi.org/10.4103/psychiatry.indianjpsychiatry_539_18

Tesli, N., Jaholkowski, P., Haukvik, U. K., Jangmo, A., Haram, M., Rokicki, J., & Andreassen, O. A. (2024). Conduct disorder-a comprehensive exploration of comorbidity patterns, genetic and environmental risk factors. *Psychiatry Research, 331*, 115628. https://doi.org/10.1016/j.psychres.2023.115628

www.ingramcontent.com/pod-product-compliance
Lightning Source LLC
Chambersburg PA
CBHW051404250726
48656CB00006B/2260